This Key Tracker Logbook Belongs To:

_____

Week starting _____

Key No	Time & Date Out	Purpose	Signed Out Name & Signature	Time & Date In	Signed In Name & Signature

Week starting _____

Key No	Time & Date Out	Purpose	Signed Out Name & Signature	Time & Date In	Signed In Name & Signature

Week starting _____

Key No	Time & Date Out	Purpose	Signed Out Name & Signature	Time & Date In	Signed In Name & Signature

Week starting _____

Key No	Time & Date Out	Purpose	Signed Out Name & Signature	Time & Date In	Signed In Name & Signature

Week starting _____

Key No	Time & Date Out	Purpose	Signed Out Name & Signature	Time & Date In	Signed In Name & Signature

Week starting _____

Key No	Time & Date Out	Purpose	Signed Out Name & Signature	Time & Date In	Signed In Name & Signature

Week starting _____

Key No	Time & Date Out	Purpose	Signed Out Name & Signature	Time & Date In	Signed In Name & Signature

Week starting _____

Key No	Time & Date Out	Purpose	Signed Out Name & Signature	Time & Date In	Signed In Name & Signature

Week starting _____

Key No	Time & Date Out	Purpose	Signed Out Name & Signature	Time & Date In	Signed In Name & Signature

Week starting _____

Key No	Time & Date Out	Purpose	Signed Out Name & Signature	Time & Date In	Signed In Name & Signature

Week starting _____

Key No	Time & Date Out	Purpose	Signed Out Name & Signature	Time & Date In	Signed In Name & Signature

Week starting _____

Key No	Time & Date Out	Purpose	Signed Out Name & Signature	Time & Date In	Signed In Name & Signature

Week starting _____

Key No	Time & Date Out	Purpose	Signed Out Name & Signature	Time & Date In	Signed In Name & Signature

Week starting _____

Key No	Time & Date Out	Purpose	Signed Out Name & Signature	Time & Date In	Signed In Name & Signature

Week starting _____

Key No	Time & Date Out	Purpose	Signed Out Name & Signature	Time & Date In	Signed In Name & Signature

Week starting _____

Key No	Time & Date Out	Purpose	Signed Out Name & Signature	Time & Date In	Signed In Name & Signature

Week starting _____

Key No	Time & Date Out	Purpose	Signed Out Name & Signature	Time & Date In	Signed In Name & Signature

Week starting _____

Key No	Time & Date Out	Purpose	Signed Out Name & Signature	Time & Date In	Signed In Name & Signature

Week starting _____

Key No	Time & Date Out	Purpose	Signed Out Name & Signature	Time & Date In	Signed In Name & Signature

Week starting _____

Key No	Time & Date Out	Purpose	Signed Out Name & Signature	Time & Date In	Signed In Name & Signature

Week starting _____

Key No	Time & Date Out	Purpose	Signed Out Name & Signature	Time & Date In	Signed In Name & Signature

Week starting _____

Key No	Time & Date Out	Purpose	Signed Out Name & Signature	Time & Date In	Signed In Name & Signature

Week starting _____

Key No	Time & Date Out	Purpose	Signed Out Name & Signature	Time & Date In	Signed In Name & Signature

Week starting _____

Key No	Time & Date Out	Purpose	Signed Out Name & Signature	Time & Date In	Signed In Name & Signature

Week starting _____

Key No	Time & Date Out	Purpose	Signed Out Name & Signature	Time & Date In	Signed In Name & Signature

Week starting _____

Key No	Time & Date Out	Purpose	Signed Out Name & Signature	Time & Date In	Signed In Name & Signature

Week starting _____

Key No	Time & Date Out	Purpose	Signed Out Name & Signature	Time & Date In	Signed In Name & Signature

Week starting _____

Key No	Time & Date Out	Purpose	Signed Out Name & Signature	Time & Date In	Signed In Name & Signature

Week starting _____

Key No	Time & Date Out	Purpose	Signed Out Name & Signature	Time & Date In	Signed In Name & Signature

Week starting _____

Key No	Time & Date Out	Purpose	Signed Out Name & Signature	Time & Date In	Signed In Name & Signature

Week starting _____

Key No	Time & Date Out	Purpose	Signed Out Name & Signature	Time & Date In	Signed In Name & Signature

Week starting _____

Key No	Time & Date Out	Purpose	Signed Out Name & Signature	Time & Date In	Signed In Name & Signature

Week starting _____

Key No	Time & Date Out	Purpose	Signed Out Name & Signature	Time & Date In	Signed In Name & Signature

Week starting _____

Key No	Time & Date Out	Purpose	Signed Out Name & Signature	Time & Date In	Signed In Name & Signature

Week starting _____

Key No	Time & Date Out	Purpose	Signed Out Name & Signature	Time & Date In	Signed In Name & Signature

Week starting _____

Key No	Time & Date Out	Purpose	Signed Out Name & Signature	Time & Date In	Signed In Name & Signature

Week starting _____

Key No	Time & Date Out	Purpose	Signed Out Name & Signature	Time & Date In	Signed In Name & Signature

Week starting _____

Key No	Time & Date Out	Purpose	Signed Out Name & Signature	Time & Date In	Signed In Name & Signature

Week starting _____

Key No	Time & Date Out	Purpose	Signed Out Name & Signature	Time & Date In	Signed In Name & Signature

Week starting _____

Key No	Time & Date Out	Purpose	Signed Out Name & Signature	Time & Date In	Signed In Name & Signature

Week starting _____

Key No	Time & Date Out	Purpose	Signed Out Name & Signature	Time & Date In	Signed In Name & Signature

Week starting _____

Key No	Time & Date Out	Purpose	Signed Out Name & Signature	Time & Date In	Signed In Name & Signature

Week starting _____

Key No	Time & Date Out	Purpose	Signed Out Name & Signature	Time & Date In	Signed In Name & Signature

Week starting _____

Key No	Time & Date Out	Purpose	Signed Out Name & Signature	Time & Date In	Signed In Name & Signature

Week starting _____

Key No	Time & Date Out	Purpose	Signed Out Name & Signature	Time & Date In	Signed In Name & Signature

Week starting _____

Key No	Time & Date Out	Purpose	Signed Out Name & Signature	Time & Date In	Signed In Name & Signature

Week starting _____

Key No	Time & Date Out	Purpose	Signed Out Name & Signature	Time & Date In	Signed In Name & Signature

Week starting _____

Key No	Time & Date Out	Purpose	Signed Out Name & Signature	Time & Date In	Signed In Name & Signature

Week starting _____

Key No	Time & Date Out	Purpose	Signed Out Name & Signature	Time & Date In	Signed In Name & Signature

Week starting _____

Key No	Time & Date Out	Purpose	Signed Out Name & Signature	Time & Date In	Signed In Name & Signature

Week starting _____					
Key No	Time & Date Out	Purpose	Signed Out Name & Signature	Time & Date In	Signed In Name & Signature

Week starting _____

Key No	Time & Date Out	Purpose	Signed Out Name & Signature	Time & Date In	Signed In Name & Signature

Week starting _____

Key No	Time & Date Out	Purpose	Signed Out Name & Signature	Time & Date In	Signed In Name & Signature

Week starting _____

Key No	Time & Date Out	Purpose	Signed Out Name & Signature	Time & Date In	Signed In Name & Signature

Week starting _____

Key No	Time & Date Out	Purpose	Signed Out Name & Signature	Time & Date In	Signed In Name & Signature

Week starting _____

Key No	Time & Date Out	Purpose	Signed Out Name & Signature	Time & Date In	Signed In Name & Signature

Week starting _____

Key No	Time & Date Out	Purpose	Signed Out Name & Signature	Time & Date In	Signed In Name & Signature

Week starting _____

Key No	Time & Date Out	Purpose	Signed Out Name & Signature	Time & Date In	Signed In Name & Signature

Week starting _____

Key No	Time & Date Out	Purpose	Signed Out Name & Signature	Time & Date In	Signed In Name & Signature

Week starting _____

Key No	Time & Date Out	Purpose	Signed Out Name & Signature	Time & Date In	Signed In Name & Signature

Week starting _____

Key No	Time & Date Out	Purpose	Signed Out Name & Signature	Time & Date In	Signed In Name & Signature

Week starting _____

Key No	Time & Date Out	Purpose	Signed Out Name & Signature	Time & Date In	Signed In Name & Signature

Week starting _____

Key No	Time & Date Out	Purpose	Signed Out Name & Signature	Time & Date In	Signed In Name & Signature

Week starting _____

Key No	Time & Date Out	Purpose	Signed Out Name & Signature	Time & Date In	Signed In Name & Signature

Week starting _____

Key No	Time & Date Out	Purpose	Signed Out Name & Signature	Time & Date In	Signed In Name & Signature

Week starting _____

Key No	Time & Date Out	Purpose	Signed Out Name & Signature	Time & Date In	Signed In Name & Signature

Week starting _____

Key No	Time & Date Out	Purpose	Signed Out Name & Signature	Time & Date In	Signed In Name & Signature

Week starting _____

Key No	Time & Date Out	Purpose	Signed Out Name & Signature	Time & Date In	Signed In Name & Signature

Week starting _____

Key No	Time & Date Out	Purpose	Signed Out Name & Signature	Time & Date In	Signed In Name & Signature

Week starting _____

Key No	Time & Date Out	Purpose	Signed Out Name & Signature	Time & Date In	Signed In Name & Signature

Week starting _____

Key No	Time & Date Out	Purpose	Signed Out Name & Signature	Time & Date In	Signed In Name & Signature

Week starting _____

Key No	Time & Date Out	Purpose	Signed Out Name & Signature	Time & Date In	Signed In Name & Signature

Week starting _____

Key No	Time & Date Out	Purpose	Signed Out Name & Signature	Time & Date In	Signed In Name & Signature

Week starting _____

Key No	Time & Date Out	Purpose	Signed Out Name & Signature	Time & Date In	Signed In Name & Signature

Week starting _____

Key No	Time & Date Out	Purpose	Signed Out Name & Signature	Time & Date In	Signed In Name & Signature

Week starting _____

Key No	Time & Date Out	Purpose	Signed Out Name & Signature	Time & Date In	Signed In Name & Signature

Week starting _____

Key No	Time & Date Out	Purpose	Signed Out Name & Signature	Time & Date In	Signed In Name & Signature

Week starting _____

Key No	Time & Date Out	Purpose	Signed Out Name & Signature	Time & Date In	Signed In Name & Signature

Week starting _____

Key No	Time & Date Out	Purpose	Signed Out Name & Signature	Time & Date In	Signed In Name & Signature

Week starting _____

Key No	Time & Date Out	Purpose	Signed Out Name & Signature	Time & Date In	Signed In Name & Signature

Week starting _____

Key No	Time & Date Out	Purpose	Signed Out Name & Signature	Time & Date In	Signed In Name & Signature

Week starting _____

Key No	Time & Date Out	Purpose	Signed Out Name & Signature	Time & Date In	Signed In Name & Signature

Week starting _____

Key No	Time & Date Out	Purpose	Signed Out Name & Signature	Time & Date In	Signed In Name & Signature

Week starting _____

Key No	Time & Date Out	Purpose	Signed Out Name & Signature	Time & Date In	Signed In Name & Signature

Week starting _____

Key No	Time & Date Out	Purpose	Signed Out Name & Signature	Time & Date In	Signed In Name & Signature

Week starting _____

Key No	Time & Date Out	Purpose	Signed Out Name & Signature	Time & Date In	Signed In Name & Signature

Week starting _____

Key No	Time & Date Out	Purpose	Signed Out Name & Signature	Time & Date In	Signed In Name & Signature

Week starting _____

Key No	Time & Date Out	Purpose	Signed Out Name & Signature	Time & Date In	Signed In Name & Signature

Week starting _____

Key No	Time & Date Out	Purpose	Signed Out Name & Signature	Time & Date In	Signed In Name & Signature

Week starting _____

Key No	Time & Date Out	Purpose	Signed Out Name & Signature	Time & Date In	Signed In Name & Signature

Week starting _____

Key No	Time & Date Out	Purpose	Signed Out Name & Signature	Time & Date In	Signed In Name & Signature

Week starting _____

Key No	Time & Date Out	Purpose	Signed Out Name & Signature	Time & Date In	Signed In Name & Signature

Week starting _____

Key No	Time & Date Out	Purpose	Signed Out Name & Signature	Time & Date In	Signed In Name & Signature

Week starting _____

Key No	Time & Date Out	Purpose	Signed Out Name & Signature	Time & Date In	Signed In Name & Signature

Week starting _____

Key No	Time & Date Out	Purpose	Signed Out Name & Signature	Time & Date In	Signed In Name & Signature

Week starting _____

Key No	Time & Date Out	Purpose	Signed Out Name & Signature	Time & Date In	Signed In Name & Signature

Week starting _____

Key No	Time & Date Out	Purpose	Signed Out Name & Signature	Time & Date In	Signed In Name & Signature

Week starting _____

Key No	Time & Date Out	Purpose	Signed Out Name & Signature	Time & Date In	Signed In Name & Signature

Week starting _____

Key No	Time & Date Out	Purpose	Signed Out Name & Signature	Time & Date In	Signed In Name & Signature

Week starting _____

Key No	Time & Date Out	Purpose	Signed Out Name & Signature	Time & Date In	Signed In Name & Signature

Week starting _____

Key No	Time & Date Out	Purpose	Signed Out Name & Signature	Time & Date In	Signed In Name & Signature

Week starting _____

Key No	Time & Date Out	Purpose	Signed Out Name & Signature	Time & Date In	Signed In Name & Signature

Week starting _____

Key No	Time & Date Out	Purpose	Signed Out Name & Signature	Time & Date In	Signed In Name & Signature

Week starting _____

Key No	Time & Date Out	Purpose	Signed Out Name & Signature	Time & Date In	Signed In Name & Signature

Week starting _____

Key No	Time & Date Out	Purpose	Signed Out Name & Signature	Time & Date In	Signed In Name & Signature

Week starting _____

Key No	Time & Date Out	Purpose	Signed Out Name & Signature	Time & Date In	Signed In Name & Signature

Week starting _____

Key No	Time & Date Out	Purpose	Signed Out Name & Signature	Time & Date In	Signed In Name & Signature

Week starting _____

Key No	Time & Date Out	Purpose	Signed Out Name & Signature	Time & Date In	Signed In Name & Signature

Week starting _____

Key No	Time & Date Out	Purpose	Signed Out Name & Signature	Time & Date In	Signed In Name & Signature

Week starting _____

Key No	Time & Date Out	Purpose	Signed Out Name & Signature	Time & Date In	Signed In Name & Signature